Women Mean Business

The Secret of Selling to Women

Judy Hoyt Pettigrew

Copies of this book are available at wholesale prices for use by sales departments and in sales training. In addition, sales training workshops on this subject are conducted by the author with the book included in the workshop fee.

For more information, please contact
Judy Hoyt Pettigrew
Phone 1-888-872-9691
Fax 1-877-705-9377
E-mail mom@wowunlimited.com

How this book came to be

As in any article, book, presentation or business document; premises, assumptions, and strategies are built on gathered data and information. Every effort has been made to insure the validity of the data and statistics presented in this book. The sources specifically referred to and quoted are listed in the Helpful Resource Section at the back of the book. However, I cannot guarantee the total accuracy of any of the geographic and demographic information. Face it, a case can be made for almost anything, by quoting germane statistics!

This book is drawn from, as well, my 35 years experience in the marketing profession, many of those years spent in organizations where marketing and sales were rivals for annual budget allocations and the relationship between the two departments was far more competitive than collaborative! It will undoubtedly come as a surprise to some of those VPs of Sales to whom I reported that I am writing about selling. Let me tell you why.

Much of my career has involved assignments where the audience (or a significant portion of it) to which we were marketing was women. Whether during my corporate years or these entrepreneurial years of serving clients directly, in my humble opinion, many of the campaigns were right on target – the right methods, messages and messengers. Yet, more times than I care to count, while the marketing yielded substantial leads, the sales outcomes were not as significant. Of course, sales pointed the finger at us and we pointed the finger at them.

To be honest, I wasn't always sure we were blameless. Over the years, I have shared that work with a very reliable panel of judges - real women - women with whom I worked, played and networked. They were blatantly honest, as women usually are, and their feedback helped me understand that marketing to women is much more than putting a woman's picture in an ad or creating a commercial that shows her involved in stereotypical "woman's" activities. What I learned was that marketing to women needs to be as personal as it is professional, as much heart as head, and needs to address benefits to her quality of life as much, if not more so than, the benefits and quality of the product or service. Knowing these things improved our marketing campaigns for clients. It still didn't necessarily increase sales. It finally dawned on me. No matter how "brilliant" and "right on target" the marketing was, it was *full of sound and fury, signifying nothing* if the salespeople didn't have the knowledge and skills to close.

Out of that "ah-ha" phenomenon was born a whole new benefit segmentation for my company -- conducting classes and workshops focused on selling to women. And as so often happens, people started asking, "Why don't you put all this in a book?"

What this book is and isn't

While I have included some statistics in the course of this book, I am not going to inundate you with them. You've read them in virtually every printed business publication and daily newspaper, heard them quoted on radio and TV and, perhaps, even attended workshops on the subject. If you missed them, I would recommend going to the Resource Section in this book and taking a crash course.

I am also not going to try to convince you that you ought to be selling to women. If your sales are flatlined or not growing as fast as you want them to, that should be proof enough because, **no matter what** your product or service is, it is probably being purchased by a woman. In the U.S., 81% of **all** products and services are purchased directly by women. This is not just food, clothing and cosmetics. More than half of the purchasing managers in this country are women and 40% of all U.S. businesses are owned by women.

While we are seeing more and more evidence, in the number of books, articles and seminars focused on the topic of marketing to women, the attention paid to marketing to this group doesn't seem to flow to the sales department. So, those of you in sales, in companies with products or services where women are a viable and, indeed, lucrative market, this book's for you. (My hidden agenda, as a marketing professional, is to wave the truce flag, also, to show that we are not against you, we are with you – honest!)

This book is based on my accumulated experience and expertise, the knowledge of many outstanding professionals, some of whom have been associates, resources and collaborators with my company, and a ton of reading! (I have listed in the Helpful Resources Section the ones which are my favorites and to which I refer or quote. You will notice there are several on the topic of Marketing. In my opinion, the information is just as germane to selling and, vice versa, for books on Selling.) Rather than just read all this information and accept the tips and opinions I share in this book, I recommend that you share it with the experts -- real women -- and get their feedback. I feel it was important to show you that this is not one woman's view on selling to women.

Take Mary Lou Quinlan, for example. She's the founder/CEO of Just Ask A Woman, a research and strategic marketing consulting firm in New York which puts a unique twist on focus groups. Mary Lou does a faux television program which appeals to women in a way that is as American as mom and apple pie. On her own television set, she gathers women together, real women from all walks of life, of all ages, colors and persuasions, and they talk about specific products and services. The programs are taped, not for broadcast, but for her clients, about whose products and services they have been talking. As Mary Lou says, "Women cannot be wrapped up in a study. Women change every day." So, statistics alone won't help you sell to women. And I really need to stop saying, "sell to women" because I agree with Mary Lou, we have to sell **with** them. We have to make them our allies.

The first step is to understand that women do not represent "new" money. Women having economic clout is not new, nor is it a phenomenon of the twentieth century.

A History Lesson (bear with me, it is brief)

If we had all paid more attention to our history lessons in school (I know, it wasn't my favorite subject either), we would have picked up many valuable clues from European women, as early as the ninth century and well into the late 1600s. These women were some of the first pioneers in the women's empowerment movement.

During those centuries, it was just as prevalent for women to control the wealth, wield the power, and drive the economy as men. Thousands of women had the opportunity to excel for one very simple reason - they outlived their husbands by many years. Girls were married in their early teens, many times to men 10 years or more their senior. A great number of these women became a widow by their late 20s. More often than not, they were awarded the right to administer the community property and were named as executors of the rest -- businesses, investments, goods and treasures from explorations, etc. There are hundreds of stories of European women who not only administered their estates well, but built their holdings, amassing such fortunes that they wielded great power, both economically and politically.

Many of these women ran businesses that included all the members of their families, sons and daughters alike. Business was a family affair. These women nurtured, protected and preserved the businesses for the sustenance of their families. (In fact, the word company comes from the Latin phrase *cum pane*, which means *to break bread together*.) In most cases, women bequeathed their estates to their sons, although some, like the women of Sienna in the thirteenth century, set a precedent by bequeathing their money to their daughters and granddaughters! Of course, if a woman remarried, everything became her husband's property, and she lost all her power. (Undoubtedly, some of them thought long and hard about relinquishing everything, once they had a taste of being treated with respect rather than as part of the property.)

What is really interesting is that there are no women who emerged as clear leaders in any business segment during all these centuries. Nor did these women march to change laws that would give them equality with men. In fact, they did nothing proactively to ease the way for their daughters or granddaughters. For all their skills, knowledge, business savvy and money, they looked in the mirror each morning and, first and foremost, saw themselves as caretakers -- of their families, employees, and everyone who derived a livelihood from their efforts -- and not as activists or feminists.

So here we are entering the twenty-first century. Among women, there is a sigh of relief that much of the hard work is behind us. The last couple hundred years have been rigorous ones for us with the marches and protests, violence and votes, suffragists and sufferers. The work is by no means completed. There are areas in the world where women are treated with less respect than were the women of the first century. At the core of a woman's being, the one thing she wants more than anything else, substantiated by numerous studies, is **RESPECT**. It is the women's anthem, just listen to Aretha!

Within this word -- RESPECT -- is the secret of selling to women.

R Reality Check
Basic things you need to know about women before you can sell to them.

E Expectations
A woman's expectations concerning a product or service begin long before the sales process begins and impact her long after the sale is made.

S Segmentations
You can slice and dice this market any way you want. However, there are 10 specific segmentations to which you really ought to pay attention.

P Psychographics
Selling to women isn't a *no-brainer* situation. In fact, it is a **whole-brainer**. To be successful you must get into their heads --- and their hearts.

E Essence
When thinking of the essence of women, it is imperative that you understand their passionate commitment and sensitivities to environment, education, and ethics.

C C's The Market
Here is the crux of the book, tips and suggestions all starting with "C" so they'll be easy to remember.

T Today and Tomorrow
Getting women as customers is only one part of the selling cycle. Knowing how to keep them is what makes this an incredibly profitable market.

Is selling to women hard?

It is truthfully no harder than selling to men. The more you know about your prospect, the easier it is to sell to him or her. The fact is, historically, men have made their sales pitches to men. What the sales*man* didn't realize and that male buyer didn't divulge was that there was a woman behind that decision. Women, because of their history, have gained great confidence and now have stepped forward to make buying decisions directly and not through men. Let's take the pulse of this market and do a *reality check* to see just how well you really know this market.

R Reality Check

A year or so ago, there was a popular T-shirt for women that said, "I'm out of estrogen and I've got a gun." In my opinion, it should have said, "I've chosen a natural hormone replacement and I've got the checkbook." Either way, no one should deduce from these statements that women have run amok. *Au contraire*, as Miss Piggy would say. She would call this the *moi* factor. Women are becoming self-centered, in the truest sense of the word -- they are centered in self. They have a real awareness of who they are and a clear understanding of what they want. The reality check here is that women have earned it.

One more history lesson. Let's look back over the last century. It is important to do this because there is the very real probability that in some families, there are *five* generations of women who are not only alive but are opening their pocketbooks and spending money.

Each generation has impacted the next and their accumulative affect will continue to impact generations to come.

At the beginning of the 1900s, it was presumed that a woman's place was in the home. However, there were women who challenged the status quo and did daring things -- things it was thought only men were doing. In fact, in 1901 Annie Edison Taylor was the first, and the only, woman to go over Niagara Falls in a barrel. She did it to celebrate her forty-third birthday. While that was a stunt to show that a woman could do as crazy a thing as a man, Alice Stebbins Wells becoming the first policewoman in the U.S. (on the Los Angeles force) was a major door opening for women in non-traditional jobs. With the advent of World War I, women entered the work world to fill necessary jobs, and even run companies, while the men were at war. Some of them did not go quietly back into the kitchen when it was over.

Politically women were on the march -- for the right to vote. Led by Susan B. Anthony and Elizabeth Cady Stanton, women rallied, found that their united voice and, finally, in 1920 won the day. It was during this period that the U.S. Congress had its first woman in the House, Congresswoman Jeannette Rankin, a Republican from Montana. In 1923 Alice Paul introduced the Equal Rights Amendment in Congress. In 1936 even **TIME** magazine acknowledged the power at least one woman had by making Wallis Warfield Simpson the magazine's *Man of the Year*.

Nevertheless, until World War II the majority of women were wives, mothers and homemakers. With the outbreak of the war, women's lives were irrevocably changed. This generation chose, after D-Day, to remain in the workplace, thus beginning the balancing act of home, work and family that continues today. The Women's Movement added impetus to the growing numbers of women not only entering the workplace, but also challenging their male counterparts for positions and promotions. This not only happened in corporate America but in our government as well. While much speculation is given today to when the U.S. will have its first woman president, most do not recall that, as early as 1964, Margaret Chase Smith was a Republican candidate for President.

Women were gaining substantial power, both outside the home and in their own lives, especially with the advent of The Pill. This pharmaceutical breakthrough gave women more control over their lives than they had ever had before. Today, while much may be written to the contrary, women are successfully balancing multi-roles in their lives. With all this history, well-documented and well known, the reality is that women have been a major market force for a long, long time. Winston Churchill was once asked if he thought that women would gain power in his lifetime. His answer was, "When did they lose it?"

Lest you think that women are not a powerful economic factor, just consider these statistics:

- Women account for $ 3.3 trillion annually in U.S. consumer spending
- By 2005 approximately 70 million women will work, comprising 55% of the workforce
- 53% of all corporate purchasing agents are women
- By 2005 50% of all U.S. businesses will be owned by women
- U.S. women-owned businesses generate more than $ 3 trillion in revenue
- By 2005 there will be 4.7 million self-employed women in the U.S.
- Globally, women entrepreneurs generate $139 billion U.S. dollars in revenue and employ over 150,000,000 people
- 60% of all marriages have dual careers
- 10.2 million women earn more than their husbands do
- 80% of all checks written in the U.S. are signed by women
- 47% of all stockowners are women

As the song goes, women are not only frying the bacon in the pan, they are bringing it home. In addition to being homemakers and working women, women also juggle the roles of spouse, mother, daughter, volunteer, and friend. Each is important to her and represents a large amount of her time. Women are in constant states of motion, and I would add, states of emotion. There rarely is time for taking on just one task or having time for a single thought. Multi-tasking is the norm for women.

The most elusive thing of all in a woman's life is time. Of all women, more than half say they do not have enough time in their lives. Trust me, shopping, contrary to comics, cartoons and TV commercials, is ***not*** the women's national pastime usually portrayed. Why would we voluntarily spend time doing something where we are not respected?

Both men and women were asked in a survey, "Who gets more respect in a sales situation, men or women?" The following three examples show that men even perceive this to be an issue.

The percent of women and men who think a woman gets less respect when she is…

	Women	Men
Going to a car mechanic	81.5 %	81.4%
Buying a car	80.9%	71.2%
Buying a house	46.8%	39.2%

Granted these are major purchases, but countless women will tell you of others, from every industry you can imagine.

In so many instances, for women, the buying experience comes nowhere near meeting her *expectations.*

E Expectations

No matter what it is they are shopping for, there are certain expectations women have during the process of purchasing goods and services. Basically, these are not unlike the expectations men have. Both expect the product or service to perform as advertised. Both expect the product or service to solve a problem.

The ***difference*** for women is in perception and perspective. For example, women perceive the value of a product or service based on far more than the stated features and benefits. Women expect the product or service to make their lives better somehow. They expect products and services to save them time, take away a stressful situation, be a pleasant experience and even make them happier. This may sound frivolous, but women, far more than men, make buying decisions using both sides of their brain. There is, as with men, the logic/reason left side decision making process, but there is also the right brain emotional/intuitive process involved in the buying decision.

During the purchasing process, the left side of the brain registers features and benefits, price and practicality. The right side of the brain searches for promises, friendliness, honesty, gratitude, sincerity, enthusiasm, initiative, and, yes, respect.

Most salespeople have no problem citing features and benefits. Few salespeople are talented at communicating the characteristics the woman's right side of the brain is searching for. For example, a woman may shop for a washer and dryer fairly certain of the capabilities she wants the machines to have. During the sales process, the salesperson who points out the time-saving, wrinkle-reducing, low maintenance durability features will appeal to the prospective buyer much more than the salesperson who drones on about fancy dials and energy savings.

Once the woman has chosen the machines she wants, one of her expectations has been met -- that the purchase will make her life a little easier. If the machines are not delivered at the time promised or she is told only that they will be delivered "sometime between 8 a.m. and 5 p.m." (a serious waste of a precious day in her mind), her original expectation that these machines are going to make her life easier is diminished.

It is further diminished if the salesperson or a customer service representative doesn't make a follow-up call to see if everything is ok. By not showing any gratitude for getting the sale or enthusiasm over having her as a customer, the whole sales process is less than satisfying for her and doesn't bring her any sense of happiness.

All of this is right-brain activity that has absolutely nothing to do with the washer's capacity or the energy savings capability of the dryer.

Whether articulated or not, a woman always expects performance, durability, and reliability in a product or service. She also expects it to save her time, make her life simpler and easier, and, yes, even bring a little joy into her life.

When salespeople do not get in touch with the right brain characteristics, they are selling to only a small part of a woman's total buying decision process. And, quite frankly, this is what can make it frustrating for men especially, when selling to women, because the sales cycle can be far more protracted as a woman gathers the facts in her head and then weighs them with the feelings in her gut.

FYI: Here's a quick overview of a few left brain/right brain characteristics.

Left Brain	**Right Brain**
Think	Feel
Proof	Faith
Logic	Intuition
Sequential	Random
Scheduled	Spontaneous
Organized	Free-spirited
Analytical	Expressive

We often read that men are naturally more left-brained and women right-brained. Whether that is true or not, women tend to engage in whole-brain activity, more than men do, in decision-making processes.

While this is interesting to note, it is not the characteristic that solely defines women. "Where women are coming from," geographically and demographically, also plays a significant part in defining women and helping salespeople target specific *segmentations* of the women's market.

S

Segmentation

The women's market, like a complicated jigsaw puzzle, can be broken into myriad pieces. The most common segmentations are age, race, and geographic location. However, these alone do not provide insights for extremely targeted marketing -- and sales efforts. Further defining women into groups offers the opportunities to truly refine sales approaches so that the methods, messengers and messages are right on target. Let's take one specific product, Long Term Care Insurance. Here's how we would begin to define the market…

Mass Market: Women

Segmentation A: age 55+ > single > no children > nearing retirement > living by herself

Segmentation B: age 45-55 > married > children > employed > caring for a parent

Segmentation C: age 35-45 > married > no children > dual professional careers > parents who are growing older

In each case, the sales methods, messengers and messages should be different because the needs are different. And even within each of these segments there is a wealth of information to be gained about the women themselves.

In their book, **Segmenting the Women's Market**, Janice Leeming and Cynthia Tripp did a very thorough job of providing valuable insights into five specific age segments. Since this book is now out of print, which is really a shame, let me give you the Cliff Notes version of what they found from their research.

1) Mature Women

By 2005 there will be more than 25 million women in this 65+ category. They reside predominantly in:
#1 California
#2 Florida
#3 New York
#4 Pennsylvania
#5 Ohio
#6 Illinois

Almost 2/3 of this group are widowed, divorced or remain single.

There are four distinct subsets of this segment (with my definitions of each):

Age acceptors - "What you see is what you get."
Age modifiers - "I'll look as good (naturally) as I can."
Age Reducers - "I gotta have my collagen and Retin A!"
Age Deniers - "I am 39."

The top ten ways (ranked by priority) she spends money?

#1 Apparel for the grandchildren
#2 Entertainment (travel especially)

#3 Cash contributions
#4 Health insurance
#5 Home maintenance and repairs
#6 Mortgage payments, taxes
#7 Footwear
#8 Adult clothing (for herself and others)
#9 Personal Care
#10 Property taxes

2) Baby Boomer Women

By 2005 there will be more than 21 million women in this group. The Baby Boomer woman has truly defined the marketplace. She benchmarks everything by convenience, time and quality.

Residing all over the U.S., these Baby Boomer women are moving into larger homes, pricier neighborhoods, and are purchasing second homes or vacation ownerships.

Nearly 71% of this group is married.

How does the Boomer woman spend money?

#1 Entertainment
#2 Food
#3 Apparel for herself
#4 Children's education
#5 Personal insurance
#6 Products and services for her children and parents
#7 Personal care products and services
#8 Automobiles
#9 Household furnishings, appliances, electronics
#10 Homeowner expenses - maintenance, repairs, mortgage, taxes

3) Thirtysomethings

One quarter of the female population is in this segment. Their universal lament is that they don't have enough time to do what they have to do, much less what they want to do. Predominantly suburban dwellers, they comprise 78% of suburban households. Their number one goal is to own a home.

Most women in this group are married (70%).

Thirtysomethings spend money on:

#1 Clothes for others
#2 Clothes for herself
#3 Personal care
#4 Food
#5 Personal insurance and investment products
#6 Education for their children
#7 Entertainment
#8 Vacations
#9 Home furnishings, accessories
#10 Electronics

4) Twentysomethings

There are more than 31 million women in this category. More than half of them live with a relative and an additional 14% have a roommate. Their #1 goal is to "have a life!"

Twentysomethings are delaying marriage with 45% of this group being single. (The median age for marriage is up from 21 years to 25 years.)

Twentysomethings spend their money on:

#1 Eating out
#2 Clothes and shoes
#3 Personal care items and services
#4 Entertainment
#5 Automobiles
#6 Vacations
#7 Weekend trips
#8 Tapes, CDs, videos, magazines
#9 Home accessories
#10 Rent

5) Teens

There are 15 million teenage girls in the U.S. today. According to **Seventeen** magazine they have $90 billion in spending power. Today teens make buying decisions that were once the domain of parents.

How do they spend money?

#1 Clothing
#2 Shoes
#3 Health and Beauty Aids
#4 Cosmetics
#5 Fragrances
#6 Hair Products
#7 Foods and snacks
#8 Entertainment
#9 Tapes, CDs, videos, magazines
#10 Electronics

This is only one approach to segmenting the women's market. These characteristics hold true no matter what the race, but race segmentation yields additional information:

More than half of all African Americans are women with 81% of them being city dwellers. Over 60% of them live in the South, but the #1 state of residence is New York, with California being #2. It is this group for which education has the greatest earnings potential impact.

There are more than 10 million Hispanic women, predominantly living in Los Angeles, New York and Miami. They are the fastest growing affluent women's segment.

Of all the Asian women in the U.S. 70% arrived after 1970. They are concentrated in Hawaii, California, Washington, New York/New Jersey, Texas, and Illinois/Wisconsin. Asian-American women are more likely than women in general to be college graduates.

One of the most talked about women's segments is *working women* and rightly so. At some point in their lives, 99% of all U.S. women will work. By 2005, 62% of all women will be working. In addition to these increased numbers of women in the workforce, the number of professional and managerial jobs they are holding is increasing also.

Working adds an entirely different dynamic to a woman's life. Now she must truly become adept at the balancing act of work and family. And, according to a Department of Labor survey, stress is the #1 problem for working women.

Perhaps, an even more important fact is that

women are starting businesses at twice the rate of men. At the beginning of this new millennium…

> Women own 40% of all businesses in this country.
>
> These businesses generate over $ 3 trillion in revenue annually and employ 25% more people than all the Fortune 500 companies combined.
>
> Minority women own 13% of the total number of women-owned businesses.
>
> 51% of those women business owners with prior corporate experience say the desire for more flexibility was the reason for leaving their corporate positions.
>
> 64% of all women 18-34 want to become business owners.
>
> Women-owned firms grew at double the overall business growth rate in the past decade and minority-owned firms grew at triple the national rate.
>
> 60% of all women-owned businesses started as home operations.
>
> Approximately 30% of all women-owned businesses are home-based.

As interesting as all these facts are, they do not provide us with the clues we need to unlock the secret of selling to women. To do that, we have to get into their heads and into their hearts. That's why *psychographics* are important.

P

Psychographics

In the late 1980s, a researcher by the name of Emanuel Demby developed a quantitative measurement tool, which he called psychographics. He used psychological, sociological and behavioral factors to create new sub-segments within markets. In lay terms, he studied values, attitudes and lifestyles to more intimately define markets. His work allowed researchers to get a more in-depth view of consumers. Thus was born lifestyle marketing.

In the early 90s, many of us were using variations of a tool that had been developed by SRI, called VALS. Their program identified nine American lifestyles and many of us in marketing used it as the bible from which we gathered information so we could create "targeted" advertising and marketing campaigns.

The trap, I believe, many (myself included) fell into over the years is that we used psychographics to totally *define* segments, rather than to use the information gained from psychographics to *refine* segments. When used to define segments, it prompts labeling and categorization of segments into niches. For example, when it was first discovered that there was a lifestyle segment that was "into" health, there was a plethora of new start-ups to provide food, clothing, exercise equipment and supplements for "health nuts."

Had marketers looked at the psychographics differently the information gained would be used to refine segments, appealing to "healthy living" which is a major business opportunity across multi segments.

The realization hit me like a two-by-four as I listened to women in focus groups we were doing for a client. These women were livid that they were being labeled "unhealthy" because they weren't "health food nuts." Whoa, I thought, where did they get that? Well, they told us. These women had all visited area gyms and fitness clubs trying to find the one right for them. At most of the establishments, they were totally ignored by the sales staff. (They assumed because they weren't already fit and trim). They were treated in a demeaning manner (if they shared that they weren't into health foods or already exercising regularly). Or they were given less credence in their desire to exercise (if their goals were not as high as the salesperson's was).

The result of our study? The client decided to open a gym and fitness center just for women. He took time with each prospective member to understand her values, attitudes and lifestyles; then had the trainers work with her, using that psychographic information to create programs, support and customer service just for her.

Today that business has been sold. We no longer have a narrowly defined health segment niche. Now healthy living is an aspect of many segments, tweaked and tuned to appeal to many different target markets.

While more and more companies are beginning to really "get it", at the corporate level that is, the lessons to be learned about getting into the heads and hearts of the potential buyer hasn't made it to the heartlands, into the trenches, e.g., the auto malls, the insurance agency offices, or wherever the selling is taking place.

Just as a reminder...

Women are purchasing much, much more than clothing, shoes and cosmetics.

$ They purchase 50% of the cars sold in the United States and they influence 85% of **all** cars purchased.

$ Half of all business travelers are women and women plan 75% of all family travel.

$ Women own more than half of the homes in this country.

$ Women are 47% of all stockholders.

☞**Salespeople are selling <u>directly</u> to women, 81% of the time.**

Let's look at it as a variation of Maslow's Theory

of Hierarchy. At the bottom of the pyramid are *Needs*. On this level a woman needs the product or service to work, to be reliable, durable and safe. Next on the pyramid is *Wants*. Women want the product or service to save them time, save them money, be easy and make life easier. At the top of the pyramid is *Desires*. Women hope that the product or service directly or indirectly will make a difference in the quality of their lives and even help them make a difference. To truly accept and embrace where women are coming from at this level, it is important to understand the *essence* of the nature of a woman.

E

Essence

Personally, I have always believed that the reason Freud asked the question, "What do women really want?" was because he was a man. Of course, there are thousands of authors, playwrights and talk show experts who have offered up answers to that question and yet the question still plagues men -- and, I suspect, even some women! Finding an answer is imperative if selling to women is going to be successful. I offer three, core tenets -- ethics, environment and education. People who are successful in selling to women, I have found, incorporate the knowledge relevant to these three tenets and understand that they are the essence of a woman's feelings.

Ethics

Women believe that business (and life) should be conducted honestly, fairly, and respectfully. In two words -- everything matters. Last year we took a very grassroots poll at all our programs and on our web site, asking close to 1,000 women to list the ten things that mattered most to them. This is a list of powerful characteristics any sales person would be smart to develop, in order to build solid selling relationships with women.

1. being faithful/keeping your promise
2. being honest/trustworthy
3. having integrity/high standards
4. being respectful of others and of yourself
5. being on time/respecting others' time
6. being grateful/having a sense of gratitude
7. being enthusiastic
8. being humble/having grace
9. being candid and forthright
10. being self-motivated/a self-starter

Interestingly, since we completed that survey, I have seen the results of several other studies conducted by leading research organizations that have had the same or very similar results.

Another poll which has bearing on this isue of ethics is the The Gallup Organization on Honesty & Ethics Poll. It asks men and women to rate professions for integrity. While you may disagree, here are the results of their most recent poll, from very high standards to very low:

Druggists, pharmacists
Clergy
Medical doctors
College teachers
Dentists
Police
Engineers
Funeral directors
Bankers
Public opinion pollsters
Journalists
TV reporters, commentators
Business executives
Local officeholders
Newspaper reporters
Stockbrokers
State Officeholders
Real estate agents
Lawyers
Labor union leaders
Senators
Advertising practitioners
Members of Congress
Insurance Salespeople
Car salespeople

I know it is grossly unfair to single out one industry, the automobile industry, to give as an example, but with the results of this Gallup poll and the statistics relating to women and automobile purchasing, an obvious picture of missed opportunities for successfully selling to women is evident. Two-thirds of the women in the U.S. dislike the automobile buying process, mainly because they distrust car salespeople. (FYI: The number of women salespeople in the automobile industry is around 8%.) Currently, women purchase half of all automobiles sold in this country. By 2005, this percentage will be at least 60%. Now buying a car is not a one-time sale. Nor is it just the initial purchase. Dealerships rely upon maintenance and repair to increase their revenue and profit margins. There is a lot to be learned, not just by the automobile industry, but by all businesses from listening to real women talk about their automobile buying and maintenance experiences.

Buying a car is definitely a whole-brained activity (both rational decision-making and emotional) for women. It provides a classic example of the process women go through (and men, too, although maybe not as drawn out or complex!) before signing the papers for the purchase.

First, women have to be motivated to change from their current automobile. This motivation comes from myriad influences -- the reliability, physical shape and attitude toward their car, the input of others about their cars, and the convenience, lack of problems and sensory fulfillment they perceive a new car would provide.

Second, they gather information both from their own past experiences (and those of others) as well as from a multitude of resources - print, TV, web, etc. Interestingly, unlike men, they do not make the rounds of the dealerships test-driving different cars. Most actual driving of potential automobiles is done with friends' cars.

Third, they tend to take time to go back and review all the information they have gathered and try to figure out alternatives to buying the car, weighing other options. I believe many women spend a great deal of time at this stage, trying to figure out alternatives to having to go to a dealership.

Fourth, once all the information and alternatives have been made and the choice narrowed, women will initiate the actual purchase process. The question is, with all the preliminary evaluation she has done, how satisfied can a woman possibly be, if she distrusts the person from whom she is going to buy the car? And, how can an automobile sales person possibly reverse her opinion and attitude, if he is perceived as not trustworthy? The short answer is he has to be selling to her long before the purchase, as well as, during it and after the sale.

Environment

Let's go back to the hunters and gatherers scenario. Women nurture things. Women grow things. Women save, preserve, recycle and restore things. It is in our nature to not only get the most out of something, we also put back something. I imagine cavemen made fun of their women for keeping all the leftover parts from the animal they killed and dragged home for dinner. Trust me, it was the woman who fashioned the skins into clothes, figured out water could be held in the animal's bladder, left over meat stuffed into the intestines, and farming tools, needles and rattles for the baby made from the bones and teeth. Recycling was not a phenomenon of the 1980s. women have been doing it forever!

It is woman's nature to enhance the environment around her in any way she can. Inside her home and out, bringing well-being to the environment is as integral to a woman's being as breathing. According to studies, 48% of all women consider themselves environmentally conscious, adjusting their lifestyles to some degree to preserve and protect the environment. A growing number of women are willing to pay more for environmentally-safe products and are voicing disapproval of those that are not, e.g., disposable diapers, fast food containers and non-recyclable product packaging. A growing number of women say they will not purchase goods or services from companies they believe to be environmentally destructive.

"Environment" goes well beyond the "green" issues of our natural world and the tremendous impact human invasion has made upon it for women. As is reflected in the mission statement of the Women's Environment and Development Organization, social, economic, and political issues impact having a healthy world in which to live. Women globally are at the forefront taking leadership roles to build a better community, whether it be within the borders of their home and neighborhood, across the borders of city, state, region or country or around our borderless world.

It is women's relationship to health that is creating more and more advocacy among women toward environmental issues and is proactively generating their participation in summits, events and caucuses focused on health problems and the environment.

From providing ingredients and nutritional information on food product labels, to the research of the part manufacturing production processes, pollution and pesticides play in diseases, illnesses and reproductive health, women are coming together through their voices and their votes to bring about change. While Erin Brokovich may be the most famous activist in 2000 relevant to health and the environment, it is a deep concern of many, many women.

Education

Women understand the intrinsic value of education in their lives. Formal or informal, overt or by osmosis, women know that knowledge is the key to survival, success, satisfaction, and serenity.

More women graduate from high school and college than do men. There are more women in many MBA programs than there are men and, by 2008, the U.S. Department of Education projects that women will outnumber men three to two in both undergraduate and graduate programs.

However, learning for women does not end in the classroom. Women come together, formally and informally, to increase their knowledge of virtually any subject you can think of. Knowledge, for women, is the key to "leveling the playing field." They will acquire wherever they can -- from printed materials, radio, television, conferences, workshops, family, friends, workers, even mere acquaintances and total strangers! In addition, they are always observing and drawing in information, almost as if by osmosis.

In her excellent book, **EVEolution: The Eight Truths of Marketing To Women**, Faith Popcorn discusses a woman's knack of peripheral vision. Maybe it comes with the multi-tasking ability or is due to hormones, as she suggests. Whatever the reason, women are able to take in information directly and indirectly. For example, women can stand in a room full of people, carry on a conversation, pick up what is being said in conversations going on around them and notice the furnishings and décor, and smell and taste the food being served!

During the purchasing process, women may come to a salesperson, armed with loads of information, but still want an information exchange between the sales person and herself. It is more than a matter of getting one more person's opinion. Now she feels she has come to <u>the source</u>. By combining what a salesperson says with all the other information and perceptions she has gathered, she can begin to synthesize everything and come to a decision. If the salesperson cannot explain the product or service in a way that is meaningful to her, the sales experience will be less than satisfactory for her.

C's The Market

As I said at the very beginning of the book, selling to women is a whole-brainer. It is important to present both logic and facts to her, as well as probe for her EQ, emotional quotient. Successfully selling to women means developing your relationship selling skills to their finest. However, skill development alone will not win a woman as a customer. If truth, sincerity and an honest interest in the woman prospect are not an integral part of your approach, she will know, intuitively, that you are only trying to sell her something (sell to her), not help her make a wise purchase (sell with her). If you really want to C's the opportunity to do business with women, we offer the following suggestions:

Convenience

No matter what a woman is shopping for, one of the top criteria on her list is convenience. Have you ever thought about what a typical day is like for a woman? A few years ago, I kept a log of a day in my life for an article.

5:30 a.m. Get up, do a few stretching and bending exercises, find my glasses
5:45 a.m. Help mother get out of bed, go to bathroom and get settled at table in her room; then go to kitchen, fix her tea and a glass of juice

6:10 a.m. Wake up kids (a couple of times), pick up clothes and check to be sure all homework is in backpacks, while I'm doing it.
6:15 a.m. Fix kids breakfast, grab a cup of coffee and empty dishwasher.
6:25 a.m. Brush teeth, wash face, dress and put on make-up while they are eating (and shout downstairs to stop picking on each other!) Oh, and make my bed!
6:45 a.m. Go back to mother's room, clear away breakfast dishes, get her settled in chair by TV
6:50 a.m. Back to kitchen to get kids to finish up, get their backpacks and walk up to the school bus
6:55 a.m. Fix a bowl of cereal for myself, eat standing up at the counter while I quick-read the morning paper
7:00 a.m. Mother's caregiver arrives. I pick up the kitchen, make a whirlwind inspection through the first floor to get any glasses, plates, etc.; then go to my office and put papers in my briefcase, stop to say good-bye to Mom and leave.
7:20 a.m. Leave house and am in car for 40 minutes during which time I leave four voice mail messages (on my hands-free mobile phone), record on my voice-activated tape recorder things I need to remember to do and buy and thoughts relevant to client activities
8:00 a.m. - noon Meetings with two different clients, using travel time to make phone calls, stop at dry cleaners and get gas
Noon Meet with group from a non-profit for lunch

1:15 p.m. Leave parking lot to get to 2:00 appointment with time to pick up prescription for son

2:00 p.m. Meeting with client

3:00 p.m. Drive home with time in car spent on phone calls

3:20 p.m. Arrive home, check on mother and caregiver; then go to home office to make calls and work on paperwork until caregiver leaves

5:00 p.m. Caregiver leaves. Get dinner for Mom and sit and chat a few minutes while she is eating.

5:20 p.m. Leave Mom while she is eating and go get kids from after school activities

5:45 p.m. Back home. Fix dinner for the kids, clean up Mom's dinner dishes, start a load of laundry.

6:05 p.m. Eat with kids and talk about their day and homework they need help with.

6:30 p.m. Kids clean up kitchen; I go and start second load of laundry

6:40 p.m. Kids visit with Gram, I do grocery list, catch the end of the news, and quick read the evening paper.

7:00 p.m. Daughter needs supplies for school project so we run to the store.

7:55 p.m. Back home. Look in on Mom, help her to bathroom, get her settled back in chair; put second load in dryer, fold first load. Kids are doing homework. Stop to help with hard problems. Work on balancing checkbook.

9:00 p.m. Fold second load of laundry and put baskets by the stairs. Take Mom's to her and put it away. Then go upstairs and put mine away.

9:20 p.m. Telephone call. A meeting time has been changed. There are four people on my list I have to notify.
9:40 p.m. Help Mom bathe and get ready for bed. Get her into bed and turn on TV so she can watch 10 p.m. news.
10:00 p.m. Start urging kids to finish up with whatever they are doing and get baths. This goes on for at least 30 minutes! In between I work on business paperwork.
10:30 p.m. Check on Mom. Start in earnest to get kids to bed
11:00 p.m. Finally! Everyone's in bed. Go to computer and start on client assignment.
12:30 a.m. Turn off computer. Put coffee on timer. Check on everyone. Take shower and go to bed.
12:50 a.m. Read until I fall asleep.

The point of my article was how impossible to seemed to find time for myself. The point I am trying to make for those in sales is that anything -- be it product or service -- that will make a woman's life easier through convenience is a blessing! However, putting the word convenient in advertising or just saying it, won't cut it. Convenience means no hassle dealings -- before, during and after the sale.

Care

Dale Carnegie said, "People want to know how much you care, before they care how much you know." If there is one bit of advice that says it all when selling to women, this is it. Women are very wary of the sales process. They have been burned too many times by salespeople who obviously didn't care or by those who faked it. Never underestimate a woman's intuition. If you really don't care about understanding this market segment and modifying, adapting or enhancing your sales approach to successfully sell to women, no amount of slick sales patter will do it. Women are learning not to only trust their intuition, but act upon it.

In order to care about a woman before the sale, you need to be aware of and adapt your sales presentation to her busy schedule.

> *Suggestion*: If you are meeting her in person, ask how much time she has to spend with you. Find out how much information she still needs before she can make an informed decision.
>
> *Suggestion*: If she isn't ready to make the purchase, ask her what more you can do to help her make her decision, even if it is to provide her with your competitor knowledge.
>
> *Suggestion*: If she is ready to make the purchase, don't make it look rushed, even though she may be in a hurry. Ask her if she has time for you to go through information she needs to know now that she has purchased the product or service.
>
> *Suggestion*: Be sure to follow-up with her after the sale to make sure everything meets her satisfaction. When you call, always ask if she has time to talk to you. Don't ever take it for granted that she does.

This last point is a piece of gold in selling to women. By asking her if she has time to talk to you, you are acknowledging that she is busy and you are showing respect for her time.

Concern

Building a solid relationship with a woman buyer means that the salesperson needs to show concern about which product or service is the best for this particular woman. Many times, women go in armed with information and research about a specific product or service, which she believes will solve her problem and make her life easier. This can be a tricky conversation with a woman because it is important not to demean her knowledge or insult her intelligence, but it is crucial to find out what her problem is and needs are. A woman may have done much consumer research and asked many people their opinions before initiating the sales process. She may be convinced that the product she has chosen is the right one. Sometimes perception and reality are not the same, as we all know.

Let's take buying a computer, as an example. I am on the road at least one week each month. I knew that I needed a new laptop because my old one had Windows 95, had no more space on it, and a CD Rom that always seemed to work when I was home, but stubbornly refused to work when I was on the road. I read everything I could get my hands on. I made a list of requirements. First and foremost, I needed the lightest one made. Second, I wanted enough memory and storage capacity to add on lots of software and still last me at least three years. Third, I wanted to spend as little as possible on it because I also needed to upgrade my desktop to be able to do at home the things I did on the road.

With prerequisites in hand I went shopping. I decided to first shop online to get the brands and models I wanted to look at in person. Then I chose four stores to visit to compare price, add-on service and maintenance contracts, and, last but not least, willingness on the sales staff's part to take the time to help me make the right choice.

At the first store, I couldn't even get someone to wait on me! At the second store, a kid younger than my son tried to sell me the most souped up model on the floor without paying any attention to what I needed (or listening to me tell him that I had no desire to learn all the "new" whistles and bells he was showing me!) At the third store, the salesman started by asking me what I did and where I traveled. He found out about my company, showing a real interest in what we are doing. Then he asked me what seemed like a really dumb question. "Why does it have to be the lightest one?" I told him about the pain in my shoulder that the doctor had diagnosed as bursitis from carrying my laptop around. He asked me if we could put that requirement aside for the moment and concentrate on the others.

It took us almost an hour, but, in the end, he had solved all my problems - showing me how I could use my laptop as my main computer, at home and on the road, working with me to configure a "network" between my existing desktop and my laptop for accessing and transferring files. He also convinced me not to worry about the weight of the laptop because he found a case on wheels that not only solved that problem, but gave me extra carry-on space. The bottom line? I wound up spending less than I thought I would have to and got even more than I expected. Throughout the entire transaction, his concern for making the purchase work for me and the fact that he really cared, made the sale.

Confidence

In addition, the salesman built up my confidence, in myself and in him. He acknowledged the research I had done, adding his knowledge to what I had read. One of the trickier points in selling to a woman is this confidence factor. We may walk into a store, exuding confidence, but, believe me, it can be temporary. More than anything, women want to be sure they have made the right choice. Buyers' remorse is almost as second nature to woman, as guilt! And, many times, we live with it, rather than returning the item or canceling the service. However, do not ever doubt that we will tell others about our bad experience, the product that didn't live up to its advertising, or the salespeople who treated us like imbeciles. Trust me, we will shout it from the rooftops. On the other hand, women do not keep a positive sales experience to themselves either. Maybe it is the novelty of it or the joy at being treated well, but when it happens we want other women to have that same experience.

Connectedness

Of course, today we have a more powerful

medium for communicating our experiences -- the internet. I believe this single tool, more than any other, has been responsible for the reawakening of connectedness in women. It has truly given her the keys to the kingdom.

Our six degrees of separation has instantly become two, separated only by an **Fw:** This connectedness goes well beyond networking. Next time you are at a social gathering, watch the difference in dynamics between a group of men and a group of women. Men, whether they know each other or not, will discuss sports, the stock market and the state of affairs on the Hill. Women, even perfect strangers, get to the heart of a topic, and the soul of the subject, discussing not only the issue, but also discovering the intelligence, intuition and intimate feelings of the others. This bonding is strengthened immeasurably by her ability to continue to carry on her conversation, no matter how many thousands of miles may separate them.

This is an awesome phenomenon to watch. Each year when I am a delegate at the Business Women's Network International Summit, I see women, from more than 100 countries, come together and begin extraordinary friendships, having found a new "sister." The electricity from this discovery is palpable! No wonder so many corporations want to become the business partners of this organization and so many others like it. They want women to connect to them as strongly as they do to each other. And it can happen, if they understand the language being spoken.

Communication

It is probably more true of women than men that it is not what we say that counts as much as how we say it. Think for a moment about any recent conversation with a woman. Either by word, look or body language she probably asked you, "Just what did you mean by that?" Communicating with a woman is a total body experience! Starting with the mind, it is imperative to have solid knowledge about the product or service you are selling and keen understanding of how to communicate that knowledge to women. The eyes are the first tool you can use in selling to women. Every sales training course reminds us that 60% of communication is non-verbal. Be observant. What is her body language telling you? Is she a willing participant in this sales transaction or involved in it under duress? Is she open to you or closed? Have you gained her confidence or not? All of these things can be determined by open or closed styles of posture, facial expressions and mannerisms.

Listening is undoubtedly the most important and least practiced selling skill. There is so much information that can be gained not only from the words spoken but the tonality. Trainers specializing in Neuro-Linguistic Programming (NLP) base much of their communications training on listening to tonality, then mirroring the tone or communicating the attitude it represents. This technique is very effective in building a significant relationship with the buyer. Women, especially, feel that the solidity of any relationship is based on another person honestly and actively listening to her.

Women react to words in a different way than men do. Using sensory words helps a woman envision the product or service holistically; then incorporating words that connote feelings will elicit more positive responses and touch the emotional triggers that motivate her to purchase.

Tone is even more important than words. If the salesperson's tone is not friendly, warm, cordial and inviting, women may perceive that the tone is condescending, patronizing, demeaning, curt, or downright rude. Facial composure and body language enhance this perception. Anything in communicating with women that indicates a lack of respect will quickly turn them off and turn them on their heels to leave. More often than not, these infractions are not blatant but subtle. Nevertheless, she will receive these messages loud and clear. She intuitively knows how she is being addressed and will react accordingly.

Courtesy

I have found that one of the most powerful characteristics of successful salespeople is their ability to be courteous. Courtesy to a woman is the *piece de resistance*. Having good manners and providing those little touches that show respect for another person have won the hearts (and pocketbooks!) of women since time began. It's the good manners to avoid interrupting when she's talking, to establish and keep eye contact, to be attentive. It's those magic words "Please" and "Thank you." It's a sense of etiquette -- and not only in words. One of the most powerful and memorable ways in which salespeople can show courtesy is through written notes. The art of note writing, once the essence of good manners, has declined so much over the years that it now truly distinguishes and sets apart those who use this tool.

The sales tool that is good to the last dot, it has a distinct advantage over oral communication. Once out of our mouths, words cannot be taken back. In writing, you can communicate convincingly and conversationally, clearly and concisely expressing yourself without committing a faux pax. Thanking a woman for buying from you or even just taking time to consider your product or service will leave a memorable impression. A note to follow-up with additional timesaving or convenience information about the product or service will be greatly appreciated. And, of course, the note that expresses that she has been missed in your store or on your recent lists of purchasers shows her that she is more than revenue to you. Notes can be used for so many reasons: promotions, personal achievements, weddings, births, kids' accomplishments, times of trauma, crisis and bereavement. Showing courtesy through hand-written notes conveys so many attributes which women seek in ongoing relationships (professional and personal, I might add!). Extending courtesy is, I believe, the most powerfully unique selling proposition any sales person (or company) can have.

Commitment

Selling to women takes commitment -- from the heart as well as the head -- and being motivated by the desire to nurture this market (before, during and after the sale). It means developing empathy for her constant tug-of-war against time, her unwavering commitment to family, friends, colleagues, and her desire to simplify her life in any way she can. Her confidence in you as a salesperson rises exponentially as you show your commitment to her.

In return, she will show a longer-term commitment to you and your product and/or service. Through commitment, the odds of her becoming a repeat customer rise and the likelihood that she will become a spokesperson for you increases. In addition, utilizing written commitments on products and services enhances the probability that she will return. (In fact, several studies have been done which show that customers make more of a commitment if *they* complete the sales form agreement rather than the salesperson.)

Common Sense

In order to "close a sale", you first have to open it. If you will look back over what you have read, you will see that selling to women is not rocket science. Just follow these common sense steps, which as a salesperson you already know in the left side of your brain, and apply them to the women's market (which means incorporating the softer side "heart" of the right side of your brain).

Step 1: Have a real desire to want to acquire women as customers or clients.
Don't do it just because the mandate has come down from the home office!

Step 2: Gain the knowledge necessary to understand this market - externally and internally.
This should be a fascinating puzzle; not a tedious chore!

Step 3: Become skilled and comfortable communicating on all levels.
The skilled part is easier than being comfortable. Once you feel comfortable, then you've got it!

Step 4: Go where the women are.
Remember, they're busy, busy people. Seek them out -- at work, at play, at their meetings and volunteer activities. Just follow those mini-vans!

Step 5: Keep in touch.
If you want to retain a woman as your customer, communicate with her regularly. She always has new problems cropping up!

T

Today and Tomorrow

Right now, I think salespeople have a real advantage over marketing people. You're out there interacting with women -- real women -- every day. I emphasize the *real* part because out of every 100 women I see each day, maybe one or two look like the women I see in ads and commercials. As Mary Lou asks, "In advertising, where are all the wisecracking sisters? The single moms? The funny girlfriends? The bigger earners? The gorgeous forty plus? And the just plain nutty weirdos?"

As I write her quote, I wonder do people maybe resist proactively selling to women because we intimidate them? Could be. When I look at women I know today, we are sure not our mother's daughters. As Gloria Steinem says, we are living the lives many of our mothers only dreamed of. It makes me think of Gerald Baron's book, **Friendship Marketing**. It is one of my very favorites. In it he talks about consumers being like the huge houseplant in "Little Shop of Horrors", (one of my favorite plays). Throughout the play, the plant asks, begs, whines, cries, and demands, "Feed me, Seymour!" The plant's appetite is so insatiable that it eventually tries to eat Seymour.

I think many salespeople feel that if they really extend themselves to women, women will become just as that plant. What a sad attitude. Selling to women is the most rewarding experience I know. I sell to women 80% of the time and, because of that, I have an address file that is bulging at the seams. These prospects and clients have become friends, mentors, resources, networking links, centers of influence, referrers, and just plain great people I might not have met if I hadn't been selling to them.

I count on them and they count on me, for much more than the programs, products and services we provide. One of the best examples of what can happen when salespeople build relationships with women was reported on in a recent issue of **Working Woman** magazine. Dorrit Bern, chair and CEO of Charming Shoppes, related how the company receives mail from customers asking for advice and help on all kinds of life issues that went well beyond which clothes to choose. Now, I don't want to diminish the effectiveness of their marketing and advertising efforts, but I truly believe these women felt comfortable corresponding with a corporate headquarters because of the rapport and relationships they had built with the salespeople in the Fashion Bug, Added Dimensions and Catherine's stores. Here is the creative, powerful outcome of the story. Ms. Bern knew they had to do something; then realized that these women could help themselves in many of these issues if they would just vote. So the company sent out letters to its customers encouraging them to come into the stores and register to vote. She said she saw three generations of one family -- a mother, daughter and grandmother -- all getting voter registration information. What a significant involvement with customers!

You don't have to wait for the initiative to come from headquarters. Get off that telephone and get out where the women are. Wherever workers are or children are, you will find women. If there is a gathering, business or social, you will find women there. Like Ms. Bern and Charming Shoppes, find out what their concerns are and get involved.

I believe it is important for you to find your own voice, too. What I mean is, you cannot merely reflect the voice of women. By identifying what is important to you, what motivates you and inspires your passion, you will not only attract women who share your beliefs, you will be attractive to women who have beliefs of their own. It is all about caring, as I said earlier. **Encouraging the Heart** is my favorite book that really gets to the heart of this (pun intended!). James Kouzes and Barry Posner are leadership developers and, while this book is about corporate leadership, its message is as relevant for an individual's personal development.

What you can do to begin the process of selling to women today is simple. Get to know women. We are not a mass market. We are individuals that also happen to like getting into groups. Our lives and our roles in them change all the time, so taking a snapshot of us won't work. Things will change right after you take the picture, trust me. So stay in touch, listen carefully and take notes. Everything you learn today will help you tomorrow, as well.

And what about all those tomorrows? That's where building the relationship, and friendship, with women enters in. We have all read and been told the statistics about complainants so many times that, I'm sure, we all know them by heart -- 4% will complain to you; 96% will just not come back. If my get togethers with woman are typical, they do tell each other of the less-than-satisfactory experiences -- as often as they can!

In surveys of "lost customers," over two-thirds of them are lost because of the attitude of the company, management and/or employees. These same surveys point out that 95% of them would return if they were listened to and their problem was solved. Women, particularly, expect salespeople to listen and to be able to do this. The role of a salesperson does not end with the "ka-ching" sound. If you want to sell to women, you must build those bridges of partnership and friendship. The bonds of a woman's loyalty are very strong.

In the future, companies undoubtedly will become more skilled and savvy in marketing and advertising to women. By doing so, they will help lay the yellow brick road for women to follow, but marketers and advertisers will never be able to make the buying experience a pleasant and positive one for women. Only salespeople can do that.

So, in the final analysis, what is the secret of selling to women?

R Reach out to her, wherever she is.
E Establish the foundation for a relationship.
S Satisfy her need to know, her curiosity, her concerns
P Present to both sides of her brain.
E Ensure a positive experience by not only meeting her expectations but exceeding them.
C Communicate with her, in every way you can, before, during and after the sale.
T Turn her into an ally, a partner, a friend; a customer for today and tomorrow.

Sing it, Aretha!
R - E - S - P - E - C - T. Find out what it means to me.

HELPFUL RESOURCES

Books

Anderson, Bonnie S. and Zinsser, Judith P. **A History of Their Own**. New York, NY: Harper & Row, Vol. I & II, 1988.

Anderson, Joanne, Managing Editor. **The Business Women's WOW! Facts.** Washington, D.C.: Business Women's Network, 1998.

Auburdene, Patricia and Naisbitt, John. **Megatrends for Women**. New York, NY: Villiard Books, 1992.

Baron, Gerald R. **Friendship Marketing**. Grants Pass, OR: The Oasis Press, 1997.

Brennan, Shawn. **Women's Information Directory**. Detroit, MI: Gale Research Inc., 1993.

Engel, James F., Blackwell, Roger D., Miniard, Paul W. **Consumer Behavior**. Ft. Worth, TX: The Dryden Press, 1993.

Evatt, Cris. **Opposite Sides of the Bed: A Lively Guide to Significant Differences Between Men and Women**. Emeryville, CA: Conan Press, 1993.

Faludi, Susan. **Backlash: The Undeclared War Against American Women**. New York, NY: Crown Publishers, Inc., 1991.

Gray, John. **Men Are From Mars Women Are From Venus**.

Kouzes, James M. and Posner, Barry Z. **Encouraging the Heart.** San Francisco, CA: Jossey-Bass, 1998.

Leeming, E. Janice and Tripp, Cynthia F. **Segmenting the Women's Market**. Danvers, MA: Probus Publications, 1994. (out of print)

Leong, T.L. and Sekaran, Uma. **Womanpower: Managing in Times of Demographic Turbulence**. Newbury Park, CA: Sage Publications, 1991.

Nelson, Carol. **Women's Market Handbook**. Detroit, MI: Gale Research Inc., 1994.

Nichols, Judith E. **By the Numbers**. Chicago, IL: Bonus Books, 1990.

Popcorn, Faith and Marigold, Lys. **EVEolution: The Eight Truths of Marketing to Women.** New York: Hyperion, 2000.

Steinem. Gloria. **Revolution from Within**. Boston, MA: Brown & Co., 1992.

Tannen, Dr. Deborah. **You Just Don't Understand: Women and Men in Conversation**. New York, NY: Ballantine Books, 1990.

Assorted publications/issues

ADWEEK

__________. "What Do Women Want?" (June 25, 1990): pp. 39-42.

Buchanan, Rob. "Girls Night In." (November 25, 1991): pg. 22.

Lippert, Barbara. "Breaking the Bimbo Barrier." (November 4, 1991): pg. 35.

Newman, Judith. "The Year of the Woman's Magazines." (March 1, 1993): pp. 11-15.

American Demographics

Brause, Patricia. "Women of a Certain Age." (December 1992): pp. 44-49.

Curtindale, Frieda. "Marketing Cars to Women." (November 1988): pp. 24-28.

O'Neill, Kathleen and Townsend, Bickley. "American Women Get Mad." (August 1990): pp. 26-32.

Marketing News

Schlossberg, Howard. "Survey: Consumers More Aware, Still Want More Info." (December 9, 1991): pg. 6.

Ibid. "Latest Trends: Targeting Consumers According to Environmental Beliefs." (January 6, 1992): pg. 5.

Time Magazine
McCarroll, Thomas. "It's a Mass Market No More." (October 9, 1993): pp 36-41
.
Women & Environments International Magazine
________________. "The Green Consumer." (Spring '92): Vol. 13, Issue # 2.

Working Woman
Butler, Sana. "Independence Say." (July/August 2000): pg.19.

Surveys
Bruskin Goldring Research. *Omnitel Attitudes toward Women Survey*. Edison, NJ. March 1996.

The Gallup Organization. Honesty & Ethics Poll. Princeton, NJ. December 1997.

Web sites
www.bwni.com (Business Women's Network)
www.census.gov (Census Bureau)
www.gallup.com
www.justaskawoman.com
www.ivillage.com
www.nfwbo.org (National Foundation for Women Business Owners)
www.sbaonline.gov (Small Business Administration)
www.webo,org (Women's Environment and Development Organization)
www.wwwomen.com
www.womenconnect.com
www.usadata.com
www.womanowned.com
www.usadata.com

and, of course…

www.wowunlimited.com